ONE HUNDRED
Words of Inspiration

MARILYN PORTER

ONE HUNDRED

Words of Inspiration

ONE HUNDRED WORD OF INSPIRATION

Copyright © 2020 Marilyn Porter

All rights reserved. All right reserved. No portion of this book may be duplicated, copied, scanned, manufactured, or otherwise used without the express permission of the compiling author and/or publisher.

ISBN: 9781733869645

Library of Congress Control Number:2019954223

DEDICATION

This book is dedicated to the millions of dreamers and doers that need to be inspired is tiny doses throughout the day. Don't stop! Keep going! You can do it!

FOREWORD

One word has **POWER**! Take, for example, the word "LOVE." That one word can stand alone and represent a plethora of human emotions when sent into the atmosphere. Imagine, then, when one person gives voice to their innermost feelings with 100 words. When strung together, they can draw you into their world...if only for just a moment.

One Hundred Words of Inspiration is the product of a **TRUE** Visionary. Marilyn E. Porter has brought together a supporting cast of women and men whose writings are sure to touch the very depths of your soul. I've known Marilyn for most of our lives, and this one thing is known for sure: She is a lover of words. It makes complete sense to me for her to compile a collection of inspirational expressions and ensure that each is precise. Although she coins herself as the "Scatter Brained Genius," it is the latter part of her pseudonym that continues to attract people from around the globe to her, well...***GENIUS!***

We all have a need at some point in our lives to be inspired and empowered. At our lowest of lows, we seek out a source of fulfillment to brighten the darkest of days. Allow this book to enlighten and speak to your spirit. When you find that all is well in your world, use this resource to speak life into another. The power of our words is never to be taken lightly. Just as sure as we can use them to harm another, *SURELY* we can reverse the course by empowering them!

Family? It's in here! Prayer? It's in here! Faith? It's in here! Gratitude? It's in here. Are you in need of a boost of confidence? Look no further...it's in here! With a wide variety of individuals who have various insights into this thing we call "life," your soul **will** be fed!

Perhaps you will read one inspirational work a day until you've read them all. Maybe you will read them all in one sitting. Whatever you need, this Spirit-inspired work has "it"! Don't let it just sit on the shelf and collect dust. Use it...**OFTEN!**

Angela Edwards, CEO & Chief Editorial Director
Pearly Gates Publishing, LLC
www.pearlygatespublishing.com
Redemption's Story Publishing, LLC
www.redemptions-story.com
Houston, TX

Contents

DEDICATION vi
FOREWORD i
IN MEMORIUM vi
ACKNOWLEDGMENTS vii
PRECIOUS GIFT 1
AUDRA BLYTHER 2
FELICIA LUCAS 3
E. ISAIAH DAVIS 4
E. ISAIAH DAVIS 5
GAIL FREEMAN 6
GENAE KULAH 7
GLENDA D. KELLY 8
KATINA L. JONES 9
MICHELLE FLAGG 10
LaCHELE JENKINS 11
NANCY WINNINGHAM 12
KEYWANA WRIGHT 13
JOY ZEISET 14
CHOU HALLEGRA GABIKINY 15
KIMBERLY NICOLE MOORER 16
CHAUNDRA NICOLE GORE 17
ADRIENNE MCCAIN 18
SHALONDA WILLIAMS 19

KIESHA LU WAN PETERSON 20
JADA SHARISE MOORE 21
SHENIKKA NICOLE 22
FAITH WALTON 23
JUANITA E. GAYNOR 24
CHRISTINE WILSON 25
AMBI SMITH 26
NELLIE ANITA WOSU 27
GEORGINA McCAIN - FELDER 28
TANDEE SALTER 29
FAITH MAKOWA 30
THERESA LAWRENCE 31
NAKKIA D. WALTON 32
NENA B. ABDUL-WAKEEL 33
SONYA A. MCKINZIE 34
JOSETTE SABRINA MOORE 35
JESSICA L. FRAZIER 36
TINA WEATHERALL 37
DR. SHERRIKA L. WALTON 38
NOVELIST CHANEA MONEA 39
ZAIMAH LATIFAH ABDUL-WAKEEL 40
GENAE KULAH 41
ARKESHIA BROWN 42
TREVION WALTON 43

NELLIE ANITA WOSU	44
SHALONDA WILLIAMS	45
THE EXCEPTION	47
REE WILLIAMS	48
JUANITA E. GAYNOR	49
CHRISTIAN J.Z. BOONE	50
TREVION WALTON	51
A SOFT BREEZE	52
An Inspirational Tribute Maya Angelou	53
An Inspirational Tribute Martin Luther King, Jr	54
An Inspirational Tribute Mother Teresa	55

ONE HUNDRED WORD OF INSPIRATION

IN MEMORIUM

AUTHOR
DONNA GARNDER
December 19, 1973 - August 28, 2019

ONE HUNDRED WORD OF INSPIRATION

ACKNOWLEDGMENTS

THANK YOU, JESUS!

PRECIOUS GIFT

(a LaCehele Jenkins poem)

Warm, soothing, a supplier of peace.
When I have fears or doubts, it comforts me.
When I feel alone, and the tears begin to fall, it
 is always there.
When I say or do something wrong, it convicts me.
 When I am obedient, I am blessed.
This wonderful gift that fulfills my every need is
 the holy spirit.
It keeps you even when you don't want to be kept.
The holy spirit refreshes us, and we are given
grace to have access to eternal life.
Do you desire this gift?
I trust him fully and will dwell with him forever.

AUDRA BLYTHER

You are uniquely and beautifully made. Fashioned and designed purposefully just as you are for your assignment in this life. You were created to do amazing things. Go forth unabashedly and unapologetically, doing, living, giving, and enjoying your life. Love and accept your truth just as you are, right where you are. Embrace change. Make the necessary adjustments along the way. THRIVE! Celebrate you and your unique beauty often. You were created for such a time as this. Remember, Happiness is contagious. Live in such a way that you spark joy in others. Inspire and encourage them to soar higher.

Audra Blyther is passionate about helping and motivating others. She is an Amazon bestselling author, notary public, and wedding officiant. Founder/CEO of Divine Treasure, and Beautiful Sisters United: Women's Empowerment Network.

FELICIA LUCAS

COLLIDING WITH PURPOSE

I got my first publishing client from someone asking me to assist them after I had published my first book. I prayed, and God gave me a specific download about my company's services. She accepted the proposal and my International Publishing Company; His Glory Creations Publishing LLC was born. Three years later, I have worked with over 55 individuals in helping them release their stories into the world! Don't be afraid to do what God leads you to do. My one yes has opened up so many doors for others. As I pursued God, I ran smack into my Purpose!

Felicia Lucas is a minister, wife, mom of 3, author, speaker, and entrepreneur. She empowers and inspires others to live their best life yet!

E. ISAIAH DAVIS

THE DISTRACTION

One year ago, I was in one of the worst mental and emotional states of my 28-year life. I had no peace or no joy, my heart was broken, and I was crushed! I was smoking weed every single day, and I didn't love anything except my children—and even my position as a father was up for debate.

My insecurities grew and could not stand the sight of myself. But one thing stood out in this season; the enemy had managed to get me out of my posture of prayer! A day without prayer.
No big deal, right?

Isaiah is a graduate of Union High School (NJ) and football player, Minister-in-Training, husband, and father of three. As an artist, I enjoy reading, nature, and music.

E. ISAIAH DAVIS

THE DISTRACTION (continued)

WRONG! One week of no prayer, then two weeks of no prayer and soon prayer was no longer my source of rejuvenation. And I had lost my identity as a son.

I am a prayer warrior.

I was a warrior that put down his weapon – THE WORD. I was a warrior trying to fight spiritual battles, with a carnal mind and in my flesh!

Today, I thank God for the restoration of *my seek*! My seek is ravenous now!
My seek is tenacious!
My seek is real!
Don't stop seeking!
Don't allow the circumstances of life to distract your seek!

GAIL FREEMAN

HEAR THE WORD OF THE LORD

The enemy set me up to fail, and at 47, I was just getting clean from drugs and alcohol.

It was a long and exhausting battle.

But God.

I had believed the lies of the enemy.
And they rendered me useless, powerless, homeless, jobless, and a complete waste.

But God.

- I decided one day to believe God;
- I am more than a conqueror, and you are too
- God is for me, who can be against me, and He is with you too.
- He will never leave us nor forsake us.

I didn't give up, and neither can you, my friend.

Gail Freeman is an evangelist, wife, mom, grandmother, CEO, certified peer specialist addiction/mental health, affectionately known as The Recovery Maven.

GENAE KULAH

DON'T DEFLATE BECAUSE OF WORDS SPOKEN IN HATE

Stick and stones may break my bones, but words will never hurt me. This statement was often made by us as children. Especially when cornered by the neighborhood bully and her crew minions. The truth of the matter is words do hurt and, if allowed to take root, will cause damage that will affect the rest of our lives. What's wrong with me becomes our internal dialogue. However, let me tell you a little secret. There is nothing wrong with you. You are fearfully and wonderfully made. So, walk in the truth of the Word, so you ELEVATE not DEFLATE.

Genae The Destiny Designer Kulah is an ordained prophetic minister, founder of The Word 4 H.E.R. (Healed, Empowered, and Restored) ministry, empowerment coach, and bestselling author.

GLENDA D. KELLY

BIG MOMMA'S BLESSING

Big Mama was a woman of great wisdom and grace. She showed her love through cooking and sharing her culinary delights. Daily the aroma of her cooking would beckon hungry locals. With sheer joy, she would share with them. I remember asking her, "WHY she gave to them"? She replied, "so you and my children's children will never go hungry." Confused, but years later, I fully understand. Her giving has OUTLIVED her, and I truly believe, the many blessings that have been bestowed upon my daughter, my grandson, and I are a direct result of Big Mama's giving to others.

Glenda is an educator, entrepreneur, community organizer, owner of Be Sincerely Yours Events and Be Excellent Business and Tax Solutions, and an administrative scribe.

KATINA L. JONES

NURTURING HEALS

Nurturing can play a significant role in developing a child's personality. Growing up as the youngest child of four in my household, the display of affection wasn't routinely shown. However, we knew we were loved because we had all of the necessities of life: food, clothing, shelter, and each other. My forever dream was to one day get married and for my dad to walk me down the aisle. On my special day, my father finally expressed how proud he was of me. Holding me in his arms and whispering softly in my ear, I love you. Hugs do heal.

Katina is a Life Coach, Speaker, and Founder of RENU U, LLC, nurturing women from emotional hurt to healing in order to fulfill their God-given Destiny.

MICHELLE FLAGG

THE ONE

Its singular, sole beginning has given me over four-hundred and seventy-five million experiences of its essence. Our number differs. If you have ever felt a warm breeze of hope envelope your soul or a strong gust of wind thrust you onward, we are the same. We never know which one will be *the* one. But each one carries a story. Each bears a song. Every one is the foundation of life's being and doing. Your breath holds inspiration. Inspiration is the giver of life. Breathe for all it's worth. With purpose and power, breathe. It just may be the one.

Michelle Flagg is a daughter, sister, mother, and friend who ministers through various media to assist women with embracing and executing God-intention for their lives.

LaCHELE JENKINS

WORTH

Warrior. Overcomer. Radical. Trustworthy. Honorable. Bravery rest on your shoulders to withstand any battle and shattering every hurdle in your path. You are a uniquely made vessel like no other to be used for his glory. Why? No-one else can do what you have been gifted and commissioned to do. The world needs what you possess to bring forth new life. You are the beacon of light to all you encounter. Reflect the image of Christ, walk in authority, and be engulfed in His everlasting love, knowing whom you belong. You are royalty; now walk in your GOD-given WORTH!

LaChele Jenkins is a wife, mother, Evangelist, and doctoral candidate. When she is not entertaining loved ones, LaChele can be found taking pictures, trying new foods, or writing.

NANCY WINNINGHAM

THANKFULNESS

As children, we are taught by our caregiver to say thank you when kindness is shown. This reminds me when I gave a child a piece of candy. I noticed her facial expression didn't appear happy afterward. She was informed by her mother to say thank you to me. Her thank you was in a slow toned voice. I later found out the child didn't like the candy. Sometimes it may not be your favorite piece of candy, but when you believe in your *thank you* and walk in your gratitude, your favorite piece of candy is on the way.

Nancy Winningham is a wife, mother, grandmother, published author, educator, and motivational speaker. She loves to share her testimonials of the goodness of God's continuous grace.

KEYWANA WRIGHT

Becoming the best, you! It takes work, but it can be accomplished. I have five steps that can help you to become the best you.

1. **Self-Encouragement** - David reminds us in 1Samuel 30:8, encourage oneself in the Lord.
2. **Be Teachable** - Have a teachable attitude. You can always learn something new.
3. **Make Changes** - Changes are good and important for developing your character.
4. **Value you** - Do you like your hair, smile, voice, or hand-written skills? Let it shine!
5. **Spiritual Development** - Develop a relationship with God.

Becoming the best you begins with you. You hold the key to your success.

Keywana Wright lives in Flint, Michigan. She is an author, life coach, and speaker. She has one daughter, Tayler Wright-Williams.

JOY ZEISET

Inspiration is the glow in our everyday lives.
The inspiration we bring to the lives of others. The love journey of inspiring others in our everyday lives.

Encouragement is living a lifestyle of inspiration.
Having a caring heart towards others is inspiring.
Find purpose in living a life of inspiration.

Always inspire others. The simple things in life are the most inspiring. We must live a lifestyle of inspiring others.
Breathing is inspiration.
A touch of a baby is inspiration.
Service is inspiration.
The creation of God is inspiring. We are created in the image and likeness of God.

Joy Zeiset, lives in PA, USA. She is #1 Bestselling Author, Minister, Wife, Mom, Health Coach. She loves writing poems and songs and enjoys singing.

CHOU HALLEGRA GABIKINY

FAIL FORWARD

Fear of failure made me burry my gifts for years. I suffered from a very bad case of "what if I failed" syndrome. Then I learned the only way to success is to fail forward.

Fix your eyes on the prize.
Adjust your goals as needed.
Ignite your passion.
Lead the way for others.

Failure is a vital step to success. Don't avoid it; embrace it. No matter how many times you hit the wall, keep looking for hidden windows of opportunities. As long as you're taking actions, you're making progress. Keep moving forward even if you fail!

Chou Hallegra is a Best-Selling Author, International Speaker, Certified Counselor & Life Coach on a mission to help people rise above their circumstances and enjoy life to the fullest.

KIMBERLY NICOLE MOORER

DON'T GIVE UP!

There will be times when you will want to quit - don't quit! You'll feel you are not worthy, and there will also be times that you feel discouraged for whatever reason/reasons, but don't allow your circumstances to keep you in a state of despair. You should know and believe that there is life after hurt/pain, but it's up to you to determine what kind of life that will be. Take your life back one step at a time; life is not a race. Some journeys will take more time than others so keep your eyes on the prize!

Kimberly M. Moorer is an author of multiple books and collaborations, life coach, speaker, and founder of Heal One Build One who currently resides in Auburn, AL.

CHAUNDRA NICOLE GORE

Hold your head up! Look to the hills from whence your help comes from. God loves you more than you can imagine. Believe in the power that God gave you to be whom he called you to be. You are great; you are powerful; you are a child of the Most High God. You have a light that needs to shine. You are a Lens of faith; you must walk by faith and not by sight. Plug into God's power, so you can empower another. Live out loud; God is calling you to succeed with the seed He planted in you!

Chaundra Nicole Gore is the CEO of LensOfFaith Speaks, Army Veteran, Destiny Catalyst, Int'l Speaker, Amazon bestselling author, ghostwriter, and motivational coach.

ADRIENNE MCCAIN

In life's journey, one of the hardest things for me to do is to leave well enough alone. Finding myself regretting my actions, while a slow-motion replay of the iniquity lurks in my thoughts, I want to change the hands of time and have a "do-over." I yearn to believe it was a dream, and I did not transgress. Reality hits and requires me to take corrective action, so I pray and ask my Father for forgiveness. Micah 7:18-19 gives us a message of hope. God who is merciful will forgive us completely and will renew his compassion upon us.

Reining from the great state of Texas, Dr. Adrienne McCain is an educator, motivational speaker, entrepreneur, and author who writes to inspire the reader's intellect.

SHALONDA WILLIAMS

Out of all of the things that I believe, there is one truth that stands out, head and shoulders, above the rest. It is that love is precious and that we should treasure it and those who give it. This has been my favorite saying since I was a senior in high school. I still believe it to be true. But, since that time, life as a born-again believer has added to that truth. The added portion is this: And to the ones that never give it, give double. For it is what we sow that we will reap indeed.

Prophetess Shalonda, known as Nspirational Treasure, is the visionary of Love Walk Outreach Inc., Certified Life Coach, Best Selling Author, and Award-Winning Inspirational Speaker.

KIESHA LU WAN PETERSON
WRITE THE VISION

I started writing at an early age, not knowing I would be here today. I never thought that I would ever become a Self-Published Author by the encouragement of one friend. I always thought I had to have money overflowing from my bank account. Here I am, seven books later; four self-published books; three co-authored and one collaboration, Amazon Best-Selling and International Best-Selling Author. I encourage you not to allow your circumstances to hinder you from accomplishing your dream of becoming a self-published author. We were not created with the spirit of fear. Write that book! Become that Self-Published Author!

I'm a four-time Self-Published Author, Amazon Best-Selling and International Best-Selling Author, Motivational INpowerment™ Speaker, and Self-Publishing Coach, inspiring others to live their lives on purpose.

JADA SHARISE MOORE

It was my brokenness that made me realize I had a gift to heal and a voice that people wanted to listen to. I began writing my truth and all the bad I went through in "love." That relationship would have never worked because God was never involved. It was during my exit where I rebuilt myself and my relationship with God, and in return, He blessed me with the kind of love I was praying for. "God does not waste our pain." So, own your brokenness, heal and become whole because you have a story and someone needs it.

Jada is a Chicago native and a woman of God. She is a speaker, blogger, podcast host, and author of Brokenness That Made Me Whole.

SHENIKKA NICOLE

Many speak about creating a "purpose-driven" life, but what does that really mean? If you are not truly submissive to the purpose, then your life is not driven by purpose. The bible speaks on submission more than 20 times, but James 4:7 directs you to the one who provides purpose for your life. One must be submissive to God, who has provided the entire life (start to finish) that we struggle to navigate and live. Such submission brings divine presence, anointing and order to your life. Once you submit, you will find your true self, divine purpose, and peace.

Shenikka "Nicole" Felder reside in Jackson, MS; with her husband, children and grandchildren. She is an Educator, Transformation Strategist, and Business Owner.

FAITH WALTON

FAMILY MATTERS

The word family is powerful and interconnected with love. A family *f*orms a strong bond, *a*llows room for differences, *m*akes fun memories, *i*gnores petty disagreements, *l*oves hard as life is short, [and understands] *y*ou can be the glue that keeps your family together. Together, these words build a strong unit that lasts a lifetime. The love of a family sees past flaws and mistakes and is accepting of each other's differences. Don't be afraid to talk to your family and express your emotions or problems, but be receptive if they have a different viewpoint. Remember: Having a loving family matters.

Faith Walton is a funny, outgoing, lovable, and successful teenager. She loves God, has a big heart for her family and other people, and enjoys writing, constructing art and tinkering.

JUANITA E. GAYNOR

AVOIDING DETOURS

Have you ever stopped to get gas? It's late, and you can barely see the signs, so you make what appears to be the turn to get back on the interstate, but you soon see it's not where you need to be. It is easy to make assumptions about the path we are on. Our choices seem right at the time, but later we discover these choices have led us away from God because they were based on our own reasoning. Acknowledge God in all your ways today. He will direct you to the desired destination He has for you.

Juanita is a Philadelphia native that currently resides in Atlanta. An established business owner, she works with entrepreneurs who are looking for solid solutions for their business.

CHRISTINE WILSON

HE KNOWS MY NAME

Jeremiah 1:4-5 "The word of the Lord came to me, saying: "Before I formed you in the womb I knew you; I sanctified you; I ordained you." And with that in mind, I want to encourage you to boldly live the life God created you to live. The mere fact that there is only one like you should be enough indication of just how special you are, just how powerful you are, just how impactful you are. God knows you, so take the leap of faith. Answer the call. Accept the assignment. The world awaits the greatness that is you.

Christine Wilson is an author and motivational speaker, my greatest delight is to see you live out loud in your God-given gifting and ability. Be Authentically You.

AMBI SMITH

KEEP WALKING

"And without faith, it is impossible to please God." Hebrews 11:6

It is rather difficult to walk by faith if you don't live by faith. Walking in faith requires tremendous courage and strength. You must be willing to be misunderstood and even abandoned. You must be willing to give up any resemblance of control of your life. Walking by faith requires you to go to a place that you do not know, one that God will reveal as you walk in obedience. The time is NOW to activate this confidence in Christ Jesus and walk like it's already done!
Amen.

Ambi Shantay is an author, philanthropist, speaker, and minister whose mission is to touch her readers' hearts and provide spiritual guidance to weather life's storms.

NELLIE ANITA WOSU

MY SISTA, MY SISTER, MY SISTER?

Sisters, as are we.

We come – in a myriad of designs, flavors, textures, hues, agendas, confidence levels, or lack thereof, desires – even.

Perhaps at some point, we will become Mama, Mommy, Madear, Auntie, Baby,

Colleague, Enemy, Confidant, Helper, Hinderer, Challenger, Gossiper, Blessed Relief, God Sent, My Woman, My Love, My Heart.

In 59 years, I've found the most important of "Sister" labels we wear is "Daughter of the Most High," there's a special reverence to this "Sister," she has been sent to all to help us see clearly and understand more fully.

I Am She. Are You, too?

Nellie Anita Wosu, "The Encouraging One," is a Minister, Author, Speaker, Publisher, and more! She advises all to encourage someone today, including yourself!

GEORGINA McCAIN - FELDER

THE JOURNEY OF LIFE

Life is a journey that every human being must make. Whether long or short, every moment leaves prints, memories, and pictures to take.

Life's journey brings laughter, challenges, and sometimes tears.

A moment given in time to experience, all through each step taken while here.

Life is a journey through every chapter and phase of inhaling and exhaling,

Creating lines of events day by day and sail by sail. The journey of life is given to us for fulfillment from beginning to end,

Capturing its very essence through every stage and the presence of its beautiful wind.

Enjoy the Journey.

Georgina McCain-Felder, BS, MA, CLC - wife of Pastor B.E. Felder, mother, grandmother, great-grandmother, *Founder of Sunshine Ladies, Inc.*, Certified Life Coach, MBMC & Lifetime Television Strong Women Award.

TANDEE SALTER

BE CONFIDENT

Be Confident in yourself and what you have to offer the world. I know, I know it is easier said than done, especially in a world where we are constantly bombarded with images and messages of what we should and should not be. However, I want to encourage you to ignore all of those messages. When God created you, he made you a unique individual, and there is nothing wrong with you just as you are. Put your shoulders back, hold your head up, and be confident knowing you are a masterpiece and there is no one else like you.

Tandee Salter is a Confidence Coach and Marketing Consultant for women entrepreneurs. She helps women build their confidence and teaches them how to market themselves effectively.

FAITH MAKOWA

Beauty is a complicated word, a word that many people don't understand. I have learned that beauty is when you accept who you are and how you look. You can experience hidden truths about yourself at the moment you accept that you are unique. True beauty isn't about face or materialistic things, but it is all the condition of your heart reflecting Christ in you and hope of glory. Your beautiful heart is the only answer to victory. When the heart is operating in freedom and peace you can celebrate life every day and appreciate everything that life has to offer.

Faith is a native of South Africa, where she lives with her husband and children. She is a minister of the Gospel, an author, and a fashion designer.

THERESA LAWRENCE

ENDURANCE

In life, we are faced with challenges we never see coming. How do you handle unexpected trouble? Jesus told us we will have trouble, but He's overcome the world. God is fighting every battle for you, and He's preparing you for greater things. You're not being punished; you're being molded for greater. Endure what you're facing because it's glory at the finish line. A runner may feel pain in their legs in a race, but they keep running for the prize. Something great is about to happen for you after you endured the test. God honors faith.

Theresa Lawrence is the mother of one daughter. She loves the Lord. She is an author, insurance broker, and hair transplant specialist.

NAKKIA D. WALTON

Having a will to achieve goals and better your life gives you a purpose to tap into the road God has planned for you. Some people won't believe in your gifts or talents, but they're not living your life. God is always on your side; He'll never leave you even at your lowest points. Trials and tribulations come but having self - determination to surpass all obstacles will lead to an indescribable number of blessings. Once you find what motivates you and makes you happy, do not be afraid to give it your all. You must believe you can't fail.

Nakkia Walton resides in Charlotte, NC. He currently attends the University of North Carolina at Charlotte. He's an entrepreneur while also being an aspiring motivational coach and mental health counselor.

NENA B. ABDUL-WAKEEL
STOP WONDERING AND WORRYING

Too often, we spin around in our heads, imagining what will happen if we fail. We worry and wonder. And it can paralyze us. Will people stop trusting us? Will people stop listening to us? Will we fail God? None of this should be our concern. God calls us to do a work. We may be called to help someone be more confident or encourage someone to be bold and brave. The truth is, we should measure success by the completion of the work. We do the work and leave the results up to God.

Nena B. Abdul-Wakeel. Mother of 2, LinkedIn Coach, and Success Catalyst. My message is "Be Encouraged. Be Inspired. Walk Boldly into your Dreams. Because You Are Great."

SONYA A. MCKINZIE

MY GOD AND MY MAMA

My mama made me a beautiful prayer cloth with the 23rd Psalm on it. One day while my daughter and I were sitting in traffic, she started blowing her whistle, singing, and asking questions. At that moment, I was tired and overwhelmed by the trials of my day and started crying. I missed my mama and wanted her to hug me. Scrambling through my purse, being sure my daughter did not see the tears, I found my prayer cloth, perfectly folded in the side pocket of my purse. Mama was not physically there but, God sent me her gentle touch.

Sonya McKinzie currently resides in Lawrenceville with her daughter. She a ThriveHER™ of domestic violence, Executive Director of Women of Virtue Transitional Foundation, Certified Trauma Life Coach, Victim's Advocate.

JOSETTE SABRINA MOORE

I often say, "Once you become aware of the mandate that God has placed on your life, you are no longer your own!" We must walk and live that every day. I share that with you to remind you that no matter where you are in life, no matter how long ago it may have been since you heard the Voice of God whisper ever so gently In your ear the nature of your calling, it is time to stretch out in your Purpose! It is time to save the lives of those assigned to you! Now. What say you?

Josette - Minister, Mother, "Nana," Woman of Faith, CEO, and yes, my sister's keeper! A native of Bonnerton, NC. John 5:19 -"Be thou made whole."

JESSICA L. FRAZIER

We tend to criticize or judge ourselves by other's successes, DANGER ALERT! Where would we be without the differences we bring to the world? God made each of us uniquely perfect for our purpose. When life takes a swing at you, punch back like Ali, dance like Ginger, sing like Whitney, and pray like Jesus. You Got this! What's inside of you matters. The world is waiting for a uniquely perfect, with purpose, YOU! Long story short, You are the only one of your kind, and you have all the required elements to fulfill the reason you exist. Let's GO!

Jessica Frazier lives in Georgia, where she's a Certified Adolescent Life Coach, public speaker, and event coordinator. Ms. Frazier is the mother of four adult children and grandmom of three.

TINA WEATHERALL

LOST

I was young and clueless. I thought a husband and children might be the answer. So, I sought marriage.

I'd never seen a healthy relationship, but I recognized the abuse right away; physical, mental, and verbal. I was lost. I was locked away from everything and everyone - including my own family. Total control and accusations of infidelity were normal.

I stayed out of fear of failing on my own. Finally, a decision was made to end the relationship. He had made the decision! Divorce is final, but it gave me the freedom to find myself again. I'm not lost anymore.

Tina Weatherall is a military brat, mother of three, Army Mom, and published author.

DR. SHERRIKA L. WALTON

LETTER FROM MY FATHER

Everything you need to succeed; I've already given to you. Encouragement you need, I've already spoken over you. Every emotion you feel, I will embrace. You will never have an encounter that I have not already answered. My love is priceless. I sacrificed my only begotten son for you. I took many lashes to protect you and walked through hell's fire to save you. You are free to walk in liberty because I paid your ransom. There's nothing I will withhold from you because I love you. I am God, your Father, and besides me, there will be no other.

Dr. Sherrika Walton is a Nurse Practitioner/Nurse Scientist who believes, "If I teach one, I will reach many." Her love for God and people enables her to reach diverse populations.

NOVELIST CHANEA MONEA

MADAM BUTTERFLY

I am a butterfly who was born without any wings. How can I touch the sky if I cannot fly?

Madam Butterfly, can you hear me cry.

Crying to be like all the other butterflies but can't see the beauty within me.

Madam Butterfly, I finally can see the light that can only be seen through the eyes of a fighter. One who can live to teach others, we are all survivors.

Madam Butterfly, I now understand. I am a unique caterpillar; therefore, I cannot fly. I cannot skip stages of life if I want to be great.

Novelist Chanea Monea lives in New Jersey with her son. She is an up and coming author who loves writing and making others laugh.

ZAIMAH LATIFAH ABDUL-WAKEEL

LEADERSHIP

A leader is someone who is looked to for guidance, someone who has vision, and is sensitive to the needs of others. In order to build strong communities, it is important for each one of us to see ourselves as leaders, in our families, on our jobs, places of worship, and our communities; that is to say, someone in our life emulates or follows our movements. And as such, it is imperative for each of us to have an excellent character of truthfulness, integrity, fairness, and moral consciousness. Without a doubt, someone is watching and following in our footsteps.

Zaimah Abdul-Wakeel has six children, is a photographer, owns a greeting card business, travels, interfaith gatherings, and a member of the Jewels of Islam™ in Philadelphia, PA.

GENAE KULAH

DON'T GIVE UP

As we go through life, we will enter a season or seasons of non-understanding. Not understanding the WHY of it all, especially when we are praying for something, we know is the will of God. We know that God **CAN,** but the struggle is in the **WILL** He. It is during this waiting period when we feel like giving up. The going THROUGH on the way to the TO. No matter what do not give up because God has not given up on you. What He says will come to pass in His timing. So, patiently wait on the Lord.

Genae The Destiny Designer Kulah is an ordained prophetic minister, founder of The Word 4 H.E.R. (Healed, Empowered, and Restored) ministry, empowerment coach, and bestselling author.

ARKESHIA BROWN

Sitting in a quiet space reflecting on all life's goodness and challenges; understanding there is a greater purpose trying to be who you are to be.

Stop
Fall down on your knees and listen to the Most High
Intertwine yourself with His goodness
Believe
He has predestined you for His purpose
Doors are opening, and blessings are falling
Walk into your victory

There is no greater reward than being the child of a God who sent His Son to sacrifice himself
Listen and wait
For all things will be provided unto you
You are set up for greatness
Follow His will

Arkeshia Brown is the Founder of Whispers of God Facebook page, active duty First Class Petty Officer in the United States Navy, Motivational and Inspirational speaker/writer.

TREVION WALTON
THE IMPERFECT HUMAN

"Not that I have already attained or am already perfected; but I press on...," (Philippians 3:12). Aren't we all imperfect, or are we imperfect because we try to be perfect? There's no need to be perfect to inspire others. Let others be inspired by how you deal with your own imperfections. Our only perfect example is Jesus Christ. The imperfect human will continually try to be exemplary but will fail every time. *"For we all stumble in many things..."* (James 3:2). Don't push yourself to be perfect or flawless to impress other people. Push yourself to be the **best** you.

Trevion Walton is a talented actor and artist with a gift of bringing joy to those around him. He is a humble teen who prays, loves God, family, and others.

NELLIE ANITA WOSU
(a Nellie Anita Wosu poem)

I'M WORKING...

To see the side of the rainbow, where the Promises of God are.

I'm working to see your pretty and handsome faces clear

and cleansed from tear stains of sorrows.

I'm working to see you grow up in a safe environment

and not mean streets that took my first-born son.

I'm working to hear your name called when you receive your diplomas.

I'm working so you can see that hard work really pays off.

I am working for us, but more importantly, I'm working to hear,

"Well done, my good and faithful servant, enter in."

Thank you, Jesus!

SHALONDA WILLIAMS

Guilt, shame, and low self-worth are most definitely enemies to your divine purpose. Their purpose is to keep you from seeing the real you by putting up this tricked out mirror that only shows you a lie. The deception appears real and almost tangible. But, today is the day that you have to determine that you will tell the three amigos good-bye. As they exit, make an inspired decision to welcome home the angels, Liberation and Peace, and make them your banner. You are free to know that you are redeemed from all things past! Feels great, doesn't it? Enjoy!

Prophetess Shalonda, known as Nspirational Treasure, is the visionary of Love Walk Outreach Inc., Certified Life Coach, Best Selling Author, and Award-Winning Inspirational Speaker.

AMBI SMITH

SAY THE WORD!

You have a right to be healed! God promised healing in His word over 2000 years ago. It's yours for the asking. If you can have it, then God can certainly heal it; but as Matthew 9 says, "Be it unto you according to your faith." The Lord cannot heal what you are not willing to give to him. Healing is here for you and for me. Whatever your need may be, Jehovah Rapha has already provided. You merely must believe. The hindrance to receiving what God has is never external. You will have what you say!

Ambi Shantay is an author, philanthropist, speaker, and minister whose mission is to touch her readers' hearts and provide spiritual guidance to weather life's storms.

THE EXCEPTION
(a Shenikka Nicole poem)

Women are typically led
by the thrust of their emotions
Which at times can make you overlook
their love and devotion
This trait can send a woman and those
who follow in a million directions
But you, Ms. Queen
Are an extreme exception

Easily perturbed
are most women in leadership positions
Anxiety taking the place
of the mission and vision
This disposition can be the cause of
A follower worse infection
But you Woman of God
Are an extreme Exception

Much has been said
of Women in high places
Too much aggression
and lack subjection
You are an extreme exception

REE WILLIAMS

YOUR GOLD STRIKE

In life, we all have a desire to strike gold. Striking gold is that thing you aspire to conquer.

If you want to strike gold in your life, do not allow anyone to give you your gold strike as a gift. You must do the digging. You must be aware of what the digging process feels like.

You striking gold will never be at the tip of a shovel that is in someone else's hands.

Never confuse a gift with a dig.

Do not allow someone to tell you about your dreams through their stories of digging.

Ree Williams, affectionately known around the world as Coach Ree is an award-winning small business development coach, two-time TEDx Speaker, and Community Giver.

JUANITA E. GAYNOR

OUT FROM THE SHADOWS

Even though I was taught hiding was acceptable, I almost forfeited my purpose. I lost myself in the crowd, and to find my true self, I had to accept and know that the story of me was needed. Coming from the shadows allowed the doors of my calling to open wide, and it has elevated to levels I could have never imagined. Even though I have been battered, bruised and betrayed, staying in the shadow is no longer an option. Guard your heart above all else, for it determines the course of your life (Proverbs 4:23).

Juanita is a Philadelphia native that currently resides in Atlanta. An established business owner, she works with entrepreneurs who are looking for solid solutions for their business.

CHRISTIAN J.Z. BOONE

You're beautiful and worth more than money. Your life is valuable and filled with purpose. If you're dealt a different hand than others, don't be sad because your cards aren't the same; In fact, be happy that they're different. You're enchanting. Your voice can be a soothing instrument of inspiration. Always speak life unto others. See every ending as a new beginning. Some will accept you; others may reject you. Most importantly, you must accept yourself. Your ecstatic behavior can keep the team winning. Your generosity is unparalleled. Your tears can make you stronger. Keep shining you are a star.

Christian is a loving, creative, imaginative young man. He lives life with excitement and enthusiasm. He's an author and allows creativity to come alive in the expressions of his drawings and writing.

TREVION WALTON
DARE TO BE IMPERFECTLY DIFFERENT

We are all different and strive for perfection. However, being different comes with a change, and change comes from adopting a Godly mindset. Can you accept being imperfect? Do you empower others to be great? Do you rob others of their dignity? As an imperfect race, we quickly recognize the imperfections of others with criticism and disregard our own blemishes. I dare you to be different. Critique your mindset, dignity, and how you empower others to excel without focusing on their past mistakes. None of us are perfect, but we were perfectly worth Jesus dying on the cross for us.

Trevion Walton is a talented actor and artist with a gift of bringing joy to those around him.

(YouTube https://youtu.be/ItePQww3MeM**)**

ONE HUNDRED WORD OF INSPIRATION

A SOFT BREEZE
(a Joy Zeist poem)

The soft, gentle breeze of nature.

The wind blows softly.

It tickles the ears, and the wind cannot be traced.

Nature is full of inspiration.

There is healing in nature.

The sight of trees, wind blowing, birds singing, and the beauty of nature. The trees release a beautiful sound from the breeze.

The sounds are so full of energy from nature. Everything around us serves a purpose.

The soft breeze that inspires our everyday lives. Nature brings much peace.

The stillness and quietness produce such calmness that flows like a soft breeze.

It is refreshing to receive what nature offers.

An Inspirational Tribute
Maya Angelou

"I've learned that people will forget what you said, people will forget what you did, but people will never forget how you made them feel."

"There is no greater agony than bearing an untold story inside you."
(*I Know Why the Caged Bird Sings*)

"What you're supposed to do when you don't like a thing is change it. If you can't change it, change the way you think about it. Don't complain."
(Wouldn't Take Nothing for My Journey Now)

"We delight in the beauty of the butterfly, but rarely admit the changes it has gone through to achieve that beauty."

Quotes extracted from

https://www.goalcast.com/2017/04/03/maya-angelou-quotes-to-inspire-your-life/

An Inspirational Tribute
Martin Luther King, Jr.

"I have decided to stick with love. Hate is too great a burden to bear."

"Faith is taking the first step, even when you don't see the whole staircase."

"We must accept finite disappointment, but never lose infinite hope."

"Darkness cannot drive out darkness; only light can do that. Hate cannot drive out hate; only love can do that."

"Forgiveness is not an occasional act. It's a permanent attitude."

"Life's most persistent and urgent question is, 'What are you doing for others?'"

"Never succumb to the temptation of bitterness."

"Let no man pull you so low as to hate him."

Quotes extracted from
https://parade.com/252644/viannguyen/15-of-martin-luther-king-jr-s-most-inspiring-motivational-quotes/

An Inspirational Tribute
Mother Teresa

"Peace begins with a smile."

"Be faithful in small things because it is in them that your strength lies."

"Spread love everywhere you go. Let no one ever come to you without leaving happier."

"We ourselves feel that what we are doing is just a drop in the ocean. But the ocean would be less because of that missing drop."

"Intense love does not measure; it just gives."

"Not all of us can do great things. But we can do small things with great love."

"Kind words can be short and easy to speak, but their echoes are truly endless."

Quotes extracted from

https://www.goalcast.com/2017/04/10/top-20-most-inspiring-mother-teresa-quotes/

ONE HUNDRED WORD OF INSPIRATION

www.ingramcontent.com/pod-product-compliance
Lightning Source LLC
Chambersburg PA
CBHW052116070526
44584CB00017B/2512